HUSTLE
Then REPEAT

I Couldn't Believe I Was Trading
An Old Crappy Farm Truck
For a New Crappy House
That Had Real Potential

Mike Bowman

HUSTLE Then Repeat

Copyright © 2020 by Mike Bowman

All rights reserved, including the right to reproduce this book or portions thereof in any form whatsoever without the written permission of the copyright holder.

ISBN-13: 979-8575775836

Photos provided by Mike Bowman.

Editing by WordEthic, LLC.

Visit wordethic.com for information.

This book is for our beautiful daughter, Brynlin.

May you follow in the family footsteps and be a true HUSTLER.

"You need to be a hustler to get ahead, and I'm not talking about being a gangster or selling drugs. Hustle, make deals happen."

Bill White

Then Repeat

Table of Contents

What to Expect iii

Who I Am iv

Let's Get Started ix

H.ungry 1

U.nthinkable 9

S.uck Up 24

T.ime 33

L.imitless 43

E.fficient 51

R.epeat 60

Now, Push Your Snowball 79

Before You Go, Leave a Review 81

HUSTLE

www.mcgeebowman.murney.com

What to Expect

My focus in this book is to bring you closer to success in every type of endeavor. Your success may not be related to real estate or to car sales, but these ideas apply to any business idea you have or temporal success you desire.

HUSTLE

Who I Am

I'm Michael Bowman. I am a husband, father, realtor, real estate investor, and elder in The Church of Jesus Christ of Latter-Day Saints.

I'm the father of one daughter, so far. I married my high school sweetheart and the love of my life, Britney. Britney and I both served full-time ministries for The Church of Jesus Christ of Latter-Day Saints.

For 24 months in 2016—2018, I served on the Cape Verdean Islands off the west coast of Africa. Cape Verde is a cluster of nine islands with a population of fewer than 400,000 people. The official language spoken in schools and government facilities is Portuguese, but the native dialect is an unwritten street slang called *Cape Verdean Creole*, a mash-up of Portuguese, Spanish, French and English. Mastering the unwritten language of Cape Verdean Creole was one my greatest feats on those islands, which helped significantly in gaining the trust of the island people. Much of what I did there was

Then Repeat

preaching and teaching the gospel of Jesus Christ, helping people get off drugs, and helping to build houses. The most rewarding work was uniting families and encouraging couples to marry and respect their spouses, and many other things that united families and benefited the community.

While I labored on the Cape Verdean Islands, Britney served an 18-month ministry in Yekateringburg, Russia. Her full-time, Christlike ministry began later in 2016 and ended earlier in 2018. She was considered a volunteer there, as laws governing religion in Russia are stricter than they are in most countries. She helped people in any way she could, with the same primary goal of uniting families and communities.

I firmly believe that most if not all my motivations and successes come from my relationship with our Heavenly Father, who created us. However, faith was not always part of my vocabulary much less my lifestyle. When I was 10, my father died of cardiac arrest. That trauma pushed me into a long, downward spiral of negativity. I began to use narcotics and was hospitalized several times for excessive drug use. I was in constant trouble with the school system because I couldn't be bothered to go. Soon, I also was in trouble with the law. I was filled with

HUSTLE

negativity and saw no way out of my unhealthy lifestyle.

Years later, at age 15, I began to come around and seek spiritual things again. That was about the same time I met Britney, who became my girlfriend and now is my wife. Just a coincidence? I think not. I began to teach Britney about my faith, the faith I had grown up with. I still wasn't fully involved in my faith at the time, but luckily, Britney embraced those teachings and became a glorious example for me. She very much wanted to join this faith and be baptized, which led to a series of more positive events and led to my activity in the faith, a much healthier, more rewarding lifestyle.

Something else significant happened when I was 15. I began my sales career, mostly selling cars and other vehicles. I would buy a car that didn't need much work other than to be cleaned out and given a good wax job. I would clean it inside and out, give the car a good wash and wax, then pop it right back on the market, which netted me a handsome profit. Those few years as a car salesman before starting my ministry at age 18 shaped a lot of who I am and how I sell. I know car salesman often get a bad rap, a rap I deserved when I first learned to sell. I admit I used to be fairly dishonest, doing whatever it took to "get it off the lot." Now, I am honest and much more open about my dealings with my fellow man.

I still occasionally buy and sell cars, a few transactions every year, but that is not my primary source of income. I would encourage you to sell in any market or product line where you see opportunities and where you feel comfortable. Whether its electronics, cars, power tools, or whatever, here's my advice: if you *can* sell it, *sell it*.

Don't get me wrong. Many people have helped me and my family on our way to temporal success. Success is not something that is done by just one person alone. Just like they say "it takes a village to raise a child," it takes lots of support and guidance to be successful in most areas of life. My family and I work hard and have been immensely blessed. I'm very thankful that our Heavenly Father gave me talents. He has given each and every one of us talents, and the more we use those talents, the more we improve those talents, the more they develop and get stronger, the more they bless us and those around us.

It's like working out at the gym. The more you work-out, the more endurance you create and the stronger your muscles become. On the flip side,

HUSTLE

the less you exercise the weaker your muscles become.

    This same principle applies to every talent you have been given. Use them or lose them.

Then Repeat

Let's Get Started

Hey there! If you and I are alike, and I think we are, you want to make some serious money. Money isn't everything, but it does provide a better lifestyle for you, your family, and your loved ones around you. Sometimes, though, it's hard to really get ahead. There are lots of setbacks, unplanned emergencies, and many other things that can get in the way of your financial or temporal success. As you read these words, you will feel more confident about achieving your temporal goals. You will find more ways to make your living situation the best it can be.

Remember that not everything you need is in this book. Most of your success here will come from your thoughts, feelings, and inspirations as you read this motivational text. Clues to greater success will come. I suggest you write them down as they occur. Keep notes on things you should do, things you can try. Write these ideas down so they are not lost.

HUSTLE

I am a confident believer that what you think about, write about, talk about, and dream about is what you will accomplish. The more positivity you have in your life, the more positivity you will achieve and attain. A penny for your thoughts? Just a penny? No, a dollar, a hundred dollars, a thousand, a million. A million dollars of potential.

Thank you for buying this book. Let's see how far it takes you when you HUSTLE.

H.ungry

I'm hungry. I'm ready to grow.

Post Malone

When Britney and I first started out as a newly married couple, we realized that real estate rental properties were a stable investment that would give us residual income for the rest of our lives. Of course, it's hard to save up a lump sum to go out and buy a rental house. It is equally hard to get a loan from a bank with only the one year of income tax returns we had at the time. We learned that most banks require at least two years of income tax returns to consider a loan.

We had found a great deal on a south-side house, the south-side being a nicer part of Springfield, Missouri, where we are from. Against the odds, we secured financing for this house, which I will describe in later chapters.

HUSTLE

This house we purchased had an interesting feature. It was a standard 3-bedroom, 2-bathroom, 1200 square-foot house. It had old-lady wallpaper, a chopped-up floor plan, pink tile in the bathrooms, and a back deck that looked like it had been rotting for years.

The interesting feature—the saving grace—was that this house had a four-car garage. Most houses of this caliber were lucky to have a one- or two-car garage. This four-car garage was split between two buildings. There was a two-car garage attached to the house, like normal, plus, a second two-car garage in the corner of the backyard. It was a four-car garage house.

Britney and I were already skilled at living within our means, disciplined and blessed enough to have frugal personalities. While our frugal natures made it easier to get by as a newly married couple with a baby on the way, this also provided more opportunity and the cash to invest in our future.

Our motto was waste not, want not. We did not need the extra 20x25 building in the corner of our backyard. Could we have used it to store extra belongings? Of course. Could we have used it as a doggy playroom for our Labrador/German Shepherd, Sport?

Of course.

HUSTLE

Actually, a doggy playroom was Britney's first choice, but we decided to use the space to increase our monthly income.

Before we knew it, I had posted the shop on Facebook Marketplace and Craigslist to *rent it out*.

LOL. Can you believe that? Renting out your spare garage for money?

I had analyzed the market for what a shop building that size would rent for, about $180 a month. That would cover our utility bill, or our groceries, or our monthly car insurance on Britney's Chevy and my Toyota pickup.

In my mind, it was a leg up to have that shop.

The minute I posted that shop on social media, dozens of people messaged me.

Most of them wanted to store their belongings in the shop and live in their RV or camper parked right outside the shop.

We were not willing to risk having some meth head from the sketchy side of town, all high and junked up in our backyard 24/7, so we kept looking.

Then Repeat

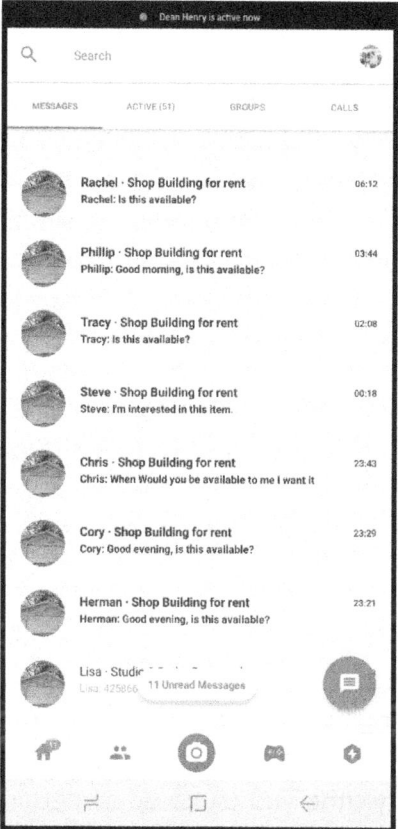

We wanted a tenant who would come by every couple months to check on things, a tenant who would store a classic car or a boat, or maybe a popup camper used only during summer. We also preferred to rent the garage to someone we knew, at least halfway knew, seeing as our first rental unit was in our own backyard.

HUSTLE

After talking to many potential tenants, and picking through many messages, we finally got a good lead. One of my high school buddies, Shane and his family, had a classic car and a boat they needed to store. They reached out to us. We talked it over and went over some simple lease terms. My new tenants decided they would pay three months in advance every three months. We shook hands, and I gave them a key to the shop.

I was overwhelmed that something in my backyard could earn us $180 a month and was even happier that I had positioned a tenant whose character I knew, as opposed to some sketchy junkie.

The funny part about this story is that there was opposition. I got comments from various people, things like "Is that guy really renting his garage?" or "I can't believe that guy is doing that." Every time you try to do something great, there always will be people questioning you, or pulling you down, people who think you may be venturing outside the realm of normal.

But what you need to understand is that there is little about you that is normal. Your potential is not normal. You are an individual who has specific talents and there are specific things that only you can do. No two people are alike, and that is a good thing.

Then Repeat

This story demonstrates that everything is worth something. That garage in my backyard was worth $180 to Shane and his family, even though it may not have been worth that much to others. There is worth in everything. Everything is worth something, especially you.

What we learn from this is that to be successful you need to be Hungry, and I don't mean with your stomach. You need to strive for success in whatever you look to be successful in, to strive for success just as badly as you need to eat. I'm sure you have heard of or watched the motivational video about "wanting success as much as you want to breathe." Watch this video on YouTube: https://bit.ly/2x7eMiU

This video and my story about renting our shop building both solidify the fact that you need to work as hard to be successful as you work for your daily bread. If you don't eat you will die, right? If you don't become successful at whatever it is you want, your dreams will die. It is extremely important to be Hungry then go out to do something about it.

Hungry is a term I use a lot when I list people's houses. As a realtor, I generate some of my income by listing people's property for sale, and helping people buy property.

HUSTLE

Prospective clients often look at me a little sideways when they see how young I am, just 22 at the time of publication. Do you know what I tell people who second guess me in the business world? I tell them I have a wife and a baby daughter, that I have huge dreams and aspirations, and that I am *Hungry*. I say I will do whatever it takes to help them find a home to buy, or to help them sell their home. Then I do it.

This instills great confidence in my clients, and it will instill confidence in your future clients, as well. Being Hungry is something that most people will not see in you at first, but when you tell them what motivates you, what it takes to satisfy you, they can be persuaded.

That is the impression that people will remember. That is what makes them commit to you. Then you feed their needs.

So ask yourself, what is one way that you can be Hungry in your business? What can you do to be Hungrier than your competitors?

Make sure that people can see that you are Hungry for success. This leads us into our next principal, which goes hand in hand with being Hungry. Our next principal is doing the Unthinkable.

U.nthinkable

To achieve the impossible, it is precisely the unthinkable *that must be thought.*

Tom Robbins

Members of my family have always thought of me as the crazy one. Usually it's for doing something funny or stupid to get attention and laughs. You may do those things, too, just for kicks and giggles. I am a fan of doing things out-of-the-ordinary, and people seem to like watching that type of stuff. In a world where there are millions of inventions, it may seem like most things have been thought of, but new inventions are created all the time.

So let's talk about the Unthinkable, about doing things that most people don't even think of, much less do, even if someone told them to and pointed it out to them. Doing the Unthinkable can set you up for success. Doing the Unthinkable will lift you up from the masses and set you on a pedestal,

HUSTLE

where people will recognize you and want to give you their business, and their praise.

Doing the Unthinkable is one of the most important things you could do on your road to success. When Britney and I were just getting started buying our long-term rental properties, our cash reserve was low and banks were not giving us business loans because of our lack of credit and lack of tax records. The cause of our hardship in getting bank loans was our two-year ministries for The Church of Jesus Christ of Latter-Day Saints, from which we had just recently returned.

I was, however, buying and selling a few cars at the time. My cousin, Dallas, was getting married in Utah, far from where we lived in Springfield, Missouri. While Britney stayed behind to work, I joined my immediate and extended family on a flight to Utah to attend the wedding, a wedding for time and all eternity. To offset some of the cost of the flight, and partly just because I love the hustle, I found a used 1999 Ford F-250 Powerstroke Turbo Diesel 4-wheel drive automatic truck for sale on KSL, a local classified ads website. In Utah.

I negotiated with the gentleman who owned the truck and talked him down to $2,700. Trucks seemed to be in high demand in Missouri, and they seemed to be super cheap in Utah. This, of course, led to a sweet business opportunity, buying low in Utah and selling high in Missouri. I couldn't wait to get this $2,700 truck back to Missouri where I could expect to sell it for $10,000 or so.

The big problem was the 18-hour, 1,200-mile drive between Utah and Missouri. The truck was going to have a real trial by fire. Would the Ford F-250 make it all the way to Missouri? The man who sold me the truck swore up-and-down that the truck would make it, "no problem whatsoever." He seemed like an honest guy, so after a moderate inspection of the vehicle and doing a test drive on snowy roads, I purchased the truck. During the rest of our visit in Utah, I put more than 400 miles on the odometer. We took the truck up into the mountains to shoot guns from the truck bed, drove some highway miles, and did some off-roading.

While doing some off-roading in the mountain snow, an unfortunate 16-year-old, newly licensed driver—having a little too much fun in his Chevy Trailblazer—slammed into the rear driver-side fender of my stationary Ford F-250. This young driver was distraught when he saw a huge dent and broken taillight in the truck fender. He didn't know the dent was there when I bought the truck

HUSTLE

a few days prior. The only new damage to the F-250 was a broken taillight and a few minor scratches. Long story short, instead of calling this young man's insurance company to file a claim, I walked away $400 richer. The 16-year-old didn't want this accident to affect his newly established driving record, and I was fine taking some cash to do any necessary repairs. I ended up not making any repairs, as the truck was not really damaged other than a broken taillight.

Counting that $400, my investment in the truck was down to $2,300. I thought I was on my way! I couldn't wait to get back to Missouri and make some serious cash profit on this truck. There were a couple of necessary expenses to make the Ford F-250 roadworthy for the 18-hour drive to Missouri. First, the truck needed tires. After sucking up to the man at the tire shop, I walked away only having to pay for three used tires. Not only did I get an extra $400 off the truck, I also got one free tire.

The F-250 needed a new windshield. There was a huge crack from one side to the other, and I knew it would not pass inspection. I needed the F-250 to pass inspection in Missouri to get the title in my name so I could resell it. Luckily, the man who sold me the truck had a hook up at a local glass shop, and I got a new windshield installed

Then Repeat

for $160, rather than $375. Another win! I felt confident that all the odds were stacked in my favor. I was confident I would soon make a great profit on this truck.

When our visit to Utah neared the end, I realized there was a slight dilemma with getting the truck to Missouri. I still had a return flight I didn't want to waste. I decided to pay my best friend, Parker, who lives in Utah, to drive the F-250 to Missouri. Earlier in the year, I had set Parker up with a girl from Missouri. We figured that if he drove to Missouri, he could surprise his woman and hang out for a few days. It felt like a win-win, and we were on our way.

Parker started his 18-hour drive to Missouri, and I headed to the airport. I got a Snapchat from Parker showing the F-250 puttering at a meager 15 miles per hour somewhere in Colorado. When I called, he said that while climbing a steep incline, he heard a loud pop from the turbo. My heart immediately sank. The truck and my friend were still 12 hours away with a truck that needed repairs. I knew it was going to be expensive, especially if a new turbo was necessary.

Luckily enough, Parker had family in Colorado who helped him tow the vehicle to safety. I frantically called around to every shipping company I could find on Google, looking for the

HUSTLE

cheapest way to ship the truck the rest of the way. After more than a dozen calls, I found one company willing to do it for $600, rather than the $1,000 or more the others wanted.

My dream of making a killing on this truck started to fade, adding $600 in shipping as well as paying Parker and flying him back to Utah. I also had the unknown expense of replacing the turbo, which turned out to be necessary. I got multiple quotes from multiple shops, all of which were in the $3,000 range. That would cut heavily into any profit, making the truck look like a break-even deal, if that. Fortunately, my friend and neighbor is a diesel mechanic, who was generous enough to do all of the work for less than $1,000. Huge success!

All in all, this Ford F-250 had been quite an adventure so far. After the truck was all buttoned up and ready to go, with new tires, a new windshield, and a rebuilt turbo, I knew I could sell it for what I had in it, that I could at least break even. But I realized that was not enough, not for me. I did not want to just break even, I wanted to make money. I wanted to score big. I wanted to do the Unthinkable. I decided to trade that old Ford F-250 for a house. Wait. What? You heard me, a house.

Then Repeat

I jumped on the MLS, Multiple Listing Service, a realtor website with every house for sale in my state. In the search bar I put $5,000 - $25,000. I searched through every single crappy house for sale in southwest Missouri that was in the price range of the value of my truck. I called 30 listings and talked to 30 realtors who had crappy properties listed. I asked every single one of those realtors if their seller would entertain a truck trade for their crappy property. I had, of course, sent information and pictures of the truck to each of the 30 realtors. Although most realtors did not take me seriously and many just laughed, I persisted.

Of the 30 realtors I called, only two said it might work. Of those two realtors, only one followed through by setting up an appointment with his seller. In the meantime, I went in person to see the 2-bedroom, 1-bathroom, 700-square foot, crappy property on the sketchy side of town that I might have the privilege of trading for.

This property needed *everything*: new windows, new flooring, new paint, new cabinets, new trim, new fixtures, new electrical, new drywall, new ceiling tiles, just to start. Holes in the flooring revealing the crawl space foundation.

There were roaches in every inch of the house and when I opened the front door, roaches fell on

HUSTLE

top of me. There were fleas biting me on every inch of exposed flesh. The yard was a mess with a storage shed filled with garbage. The bathroom leaked everywhere. There were roaches and all sorts of insects in the kitchen cabinets and holes in the wall.

To top it off, the rotted front porch was close to collapse and might fall over any minute. This crappy home was the ultimate fixer upper. It was 700 square feet of gross and utter disgust. I rushed home to shower as soon as I left the property, afraid I'd scatter bed bugs throughout my car and house.

Even with all that, though, I knew this trade would be a step up from a depreciating vehicle to an appreciating property.

After three months of negotiation, we finally reached an agreement to trade my truck for this little crappy house. I was overjoyed with a huge smile when I received the phone call saying that the seller would do the deal.

I could not believe I was trading an old crappy farm truck for an old crappy house that had real potential to be fixed and rented or fixed and flipped.

Then Repeat

What a day that was. It took months of effort, but I had done the Unthinkable. Many people never would have dreamed it was possible to trade an old farm truck for an appreciating property. Honestly, I could hardly believe it myself. When closing day came, I signed the truck title over to the seller and I received the warranty deed of the little house. I was the property owner.

Over the next two months I remodeled and completely revamped that little house, including:

new energy efficient double pane vinyl windows;

HUSTLE

new vinyl plank waterproof flooring throughout the house;

a new kitchen with new cabinets and a new sink;

a new bathroom vanity;

a new shower insert;

energy efficient new exterior/interior doors;

a new carport with a metal roof;

a new front porch with a metal roof;

a thorough cleanup of the yard, front and back;

new trim throughout the house;

new paint throughout the house;

a new breaker box;

new switches and plugs throughout the house;

new light fixtures throughout the house;

updated plumbing/sewer.

This was a virtually new house once I was done. I had effectively turned an initial investment of only $2,300 in a Ford F-250 truck into a remodeled house that was either rent ready or ready to flip and make a profit. It was ready for the rental market, but I started to wonder what quality of renters I would get on this sketchy side of town.

This neighborhood was known to be burdened with crime and drug problems. Nevertheless, I put the house up for rent and stuck a big sign in the yard with my phone number.

Over the next 30 days, I got more than two dozen calls from potential renters, all of whom were either felons or had previous evictions. That's not the kind of tenant I wanted to keep in my portfolio, so I sold the property and cashed out all the equity I had in it. With that money, I proceeded to buy a cleaner and nicer investment property in a better part of town.

It's Unthinkable that someone could trade a truck for a house. It was not something I had planned, but once the idea struck it carried a momentum of its own, through all the ups and downs. It was never easy but doing the Unthinkable never is easy.

I can't tell you how happy I am I did it, though. I was so happy I decided to do it a second time, except I wouldn't be satisfied trading a truck for just one house. I went for two houses. You heard me. Two houses.

HUSTLE

This is how I did it. I got back on the MLS website and called every single one of the crappy properties listed for sale less than $30,000.

Out of the many, many realtors I contacted, only one took me seriously. That one realtor and I debated and negotiated back-and-forth for days, she on behalf of her seller, and me for myself.

At the end of the negotiation, I had convinced this seller/landlord to trade his last two vacant rental properties for my 2007 Toyota Tundra 4-wheel-drive automatic truck, my personal vehicle at the time.

Then Repeat

I had caught this landlord at just the right time, where he was too fed up to remodel these two crappy rental houses, which the previous tenants had trashed. I, on the other hand, had all the energy and skill necessary to remodel then either rent or flip. I couldn't believe it. Again, I was on top of the world, trading a depreciating asset for two appreciating assets. I was extremely happy at the outcome of this second truck trade for two crappy houses, even though they were on the sketchy side of town.

On these second two houses, I ended up not making any repairs. I just got in there and cleared

HUSTLE

out all the crap from both houses, lots of grubby, bug-ridden furniture, inappropriate magazines, cigarette butts and alcohol bottles, and pile after pile of trash. After a couple of days of work and making several trips to the dump, these properties were clean and no longer an eye sore. We even mowed the grass to give them extra curb appeal.

I decided to put them back on the market and sell them for cash. Granted, there were still many repairs to be done on these two homes, but they looked a whole lot more appealing now. Just a few weeks later, I accepted cash offers for both of those crappy houses, and I cashed out my equity.

To sum this all up, in the space of a couple of months I did what was Unthinkable. I traded two trucks for three houses. You don't always need lots of cash on hand to get into the business you are looking grow. More than likely you have something you can trade that will further your business.

Everything is worth something, right? Never forget that. Everything you own is worth something to someone else. One man's trash is another man's treasure, as they say.

You can do the Unthinkable! You can trade trucks for houses, you can do anything you set

Then Repeat

your mind to. There is no limit to what you can think, therefore, there is no limit to what you can do. Remember Kyle MacDonald, who traded a little red paperclip for a house?

What is an example of something Unthinkable that you can do? What is a way you can start or expand your business that may be unorthodox or out of your comfort zone?

Find something Unthinkable that you can do—then do it. I believe in you, and you should believe in yourself.

If being a Suck up seems Unthinkable to you, then read on.

HUSTLE

S.uck Up

A person who acts favorably to his or her peers to gain stasis or fancy that will eventually be used to their advantage such as a raise, or promotion, or acceptance in a group. Usually brownnosers will do anything to gain the approval of their person of choice.

Urban Dictionary

Getting ahead in life often requires money, which can be hard because most of us don't have money when starting out. That's why I traded trucks for houses early in my career. Regardless of the business you want to start or be part of, regardless of the dreams and aspirations you have, you will need at least a little capital. We traded trucks, yes, but trucks can only get you so far in trading up. We realized that money would be needed to further the real estate empire we envisioned.

Then Repeat

We also learned that a cash offer is more appealing to a seller of real estate than is a bank loan offer. We figured out, as many people have, that if we made an offer to purchase real estate and the offer was CASH, AS IS, NO CONTINGENCIES, NO INSPECTIONS, CLOSE VERY QUICKLY, that our offer was much more likely to be accepted than a standard bank loan offer with contingencies and inspections.

The tough part for Britney and me was that we were unable to qualify for a standard bank loan because we did not have the minimum two years of income tax returns, and our credit was nonexistent. We had cash from selling the three houses we traded for, but that was not enough to purchase all the real estate deals we had our eyes on. Banks usually look at your credit rating, Income tax returns, expenses, and debt-to-income ratio before they will even administer a prequalification form.

So my wife and I struggled to start our dream of owning many rental properties and gaining the residual income that came with it. With nothing better to do, we started making offers on property without knowing where the cash or financing would come from. Seriously. I figured that if I had a house under contract, with an accepted offer, it would motivate me to find a way to get the funds,

HUSTLE

one way or another, to make the deal work. It was a trial-by-fire type of deal, where we purposefully set the ends in place then struggled to find and justify the means.

Following these hollow offers, I began begging every bank in town to loan us money. I talked to big banks, small banks, medium-sized banks, banks where I had friends, banks where I knew nobody, banks where I had checking accounts, and banks I had never even heard of until I researched them on Google. Every time I went to a bank I got the same story, that Britney and I didn't have the income tax returns or credit necessary to qualify for a loan of any type.

After many months of talking to many banks, and having my credit run numerous times, which I'm sure did not help my cause, I felt discouraged. I thought I had done everything necessary, but I was not getting the results.

Have you ever felt that way? Have you ever thought you've done more than you needed to and you still haven't gotten what you wanted? I was frustrated and, frankly, a little fed up with the situation. I decided to try one more time, just one more bank, a small institution called Peoples Community Bank. I had heard nothing special about this bank, just that they were a local bank, which meant a slightly higher chance of loaning money to a hometown boy.

I walked to the loan officer's desk, acting confident to the point of arrogance, cocky, my wife would have said. I did my best to butter up that loan officer. That's right, I did my best to Suck up. Although brownnosers get a bad rap, we all know that the nicer you are to someone, the more likely they are to help with what you need. That doesn't mean we should just look at people as mere assets for our personal use. We should look at and treat everyone as human beings with needs and feelings of their own. However, if you use your words right, and use your smile right, and say the right things, and do the right things, you have a much better chance of getting the success you desire. What's that old saying about getting more with honey than with vinegar? I realized during that interview with that loan officer that the more I could Suck up to her, to say and do the right things, the more likely I would be to get what I needed, which was money *right now*.

I laid out my business plan for this loan officer and explained that I will be worth millions someday, but I needed some money to start out now. I emphasized that I had three good deals going and all I needed was the cash to finance

HUSTLE

them. I came on very confident, wholly self-assured. I left all the information, including a personal financial statement, with this loan officer, then strutted out. I did my cocky best and left the rest to God.

Although I had told the loan officer about all three properties, one stood out as a far better deal than the others.

A few days later, I got a call that changed everything for us, exponentially, jump starting our real estate business by months or maybe even years. The loan officer, recognizing that I was a motivated, Hungry young man, recently married, with some great deals on my plate, said she would take a chance on me, but on only one of the properties. She just wanted the cream of the crop, the one property that was the best deal. Okay! What else could I say, right? Beggars can't be choosers. I was ecstatic.

We agreed to the offered terms and set it up as a 15-year fixed loan. Granted, the interest rate was going to be higher because I was a higher risk, but I was lucky to get any type of loan in the first place. I had failed so often in getting a bank loan during that six months of searching that I honestly couldn't believe this was finally happening.

Then Repeat

Imagine working on something for half a year and you finally get the result you worked for. That is success. That is making things happen.

Getting that first bank loan was so crucial because once one bank loans you money, the other banks won't be as resistant. Once someone takes a chance on you, other banks and entities and people are less likely to second guess you and your potential for success.

A few weeks later, and a large amount of closing costs later, I had the money I needed to solidify a great deal. At last, all the hard work was paying off. Even though my annual interest rate,

HUSTLE

APR, was higher, and my initial closing costs to create this loan were higher, and the loan amount wasn't quite as high as I initially begged for, I was happy. It was enough, a good stepping-stone that would lead to other open doors to more money in the future, more money that would fuel my goal of owning many rental properties.

Your dream, your goal, may not be in real estate or rentals, and that's quite alright. What your goal will need is some sort of financing for your start-up or growth, so learn to strut outside your comfort zone sometimes. Learn to be a Suck up to get what you need, then work like crazy to get it done.

After that first loan with Peoples Community Bank, I reached out to many other banks and individuals who had money. I practically flaunted the fact that Peoples Community Bank had loaned me money, and that others would be right in doing so. I floated out the fact that I wanted to borrow more money through real-estate community grapevines in Springfield. I posted it on social media. I contacted people who had money and offered to pay them interest on a personal loan. I called real estate investors who owned and managed rental properties and made it known that I would gladly pay them interest on money lent to me.

Then Repeat

Sure enough, after another six months of doing what I do best, Hustling around to make stuff happen, I had three private-party individuals financing me out money for interest. And you better believe that I Sucked up to every single one of them. I was on my best behavior, with a big ol' smile on my face, showing my best self to them, and showing them my worth. I did my best to Suck up and brownnose and make these people who had money like me and trust me so they would help me and my business grow.

I used my first loan from Peoples Community Bank to justify that I was a good investment for anybody willing to loan out money. You better believe I had a lot of good things to say when it came to talking about that first loan at Peoples Community Bank. It had been almost a year since

HUSTLE

I first sought financing for my operation, and now I not only had one bank loan, but three other hard-money loans from private-party lenders.

All in all, most people are nicer to you and give you what you want more easily when you Suck up to them. What you will probably realize when you Suck up is that some day in the not too distant future you may have a young guy or girl come Suck up to you and want money from you to start and grow a business. You might be the answer to someone's prayers and problems in the future. Be ready.

I would not be where I am today without Sucking up and brownnosing my way to success. How much do you want your success? Are you willing to Suck up to the people who can help you for your success? Are you willing to invest that Time?

T.ime

Until now you've probably heard the terms 'investing' and 'return on investment' only in relation to money. However, you have to start applying these concepts to Time, as well. Make wise Time investments and then enjoy the positive returns that you receive on your investment.

Marelisa Fábrega

    As Britney and I continued our real estate investing—growing our business—we realized that a smart move would be to diversify. Diversity can apply to most types of business and is crucial for you to survive the high and the low points of your business. Diversifying your investment or your product is a smart way to stay afloat when some of your other investments are not doing so well. This is why many people who use the stock market and crypto currency diversify their investments. All our rental houses were just that,

HUSTLE

rental houses. All we had were single-family homes that we rented to long-term tenants. We had not yet dabbled into Airbnb or the Vrbo homes, nor did we own any multi-family or other types of real estate.

I started to do my research and figure out what the next best business step was for us. You will do your own due diligence in your own business and growing your product. You will figure out the best way for you to diversify your investment.

After reading many blogs online, talking to many real estate investors, and driving around town and analyzing the real estate market, I concluded that the best next step for us in our situation was to buy a mini-storage facility. This was way out of my comfort zone, a type of real estate I had not dealt with. A mini-storage facility would involve more tenants, with a lower rent per-month/per-tenant compared to a single-family home. It would be different, yes, but at the same time it would just be another rental property, which is what we were used to.

I looked on the realtor websites in southwest Missouri to find a suitable mini-storage facility for sale. After combing through all the listings within a 200-mile radius of my home, I found there were virtually none on the market at that time in my area. I was completely blown away. This lack of inventory strengthened my already strong desire to purchase a mini-storage facility. Mini-storage facilities must be a good investment if none of these owners wanted to sell theirs. It seemed everyone was holding on to their mini-storage facilities, a good sign.

It all started coming together in my mind: a metal building with virtually no repairs or upkeep, coupled with tenants on autopay, would make a mini-storage facility a hassle-free business, not to mention the dirt-cheap annual insurance premiums, extremely low annual electric bill, and rock-bottom property taxes. Purchasing a mini-storage facility was a complete no-brainer.

This is just what you may be thinking right now about your next diversification in your business or product. You may have just had an epiphany—that A-HA moment—and found your next no-brainer diversification step.

My only predicament with the mini-storage facility was that even though I had committed to purchasing one, and even though I had analyzed the numbers and concluded that it was a good investment for us, there were no storage facilities for sale. That presented a problem, but like all problems, there was a solution. My solution was fairly simple, but very time consuming. As I thought about a solution, a phrase I have known

HUSTLE

and loved for years came to mind: "Everything is for sale." This rang true to the current situation.

I decided to drive around town and the surrounding areas to look at every mini-storage facility I could find. I didn't just look at them. I called the number on every sign and talked to every facility owner to make an offer to purchase their property. I spent many hours over many days doing this.

As you would expect, since there were no For Sale signs on any of these properties, mostly what I received was hearty rejection. These people loved their mini-storage facilities. They didn't want to sell. Mini-storage facilities were a great investment for them, obviously, so there was no way they would let go of these properties, most of which they had owned for years. I persisted, calling most of those owners multiple times, asking them to sell. One owner cussed me out, another ran me off her property, but the majority never even returned my calls.

After all these calls, after all this Time, it looked as though it finally would pay off. One off-market facility finally made a counteroffer to my original offer. We went back and forth for weeks, trying to make a reasonable deal. We could not come to an agreement because I was unwilling to pay more than the property was worth.

Then Repeat

At this point, my enthusiasm had kind of fizzled out. I had spent so much Time but had nothing to show for it. You've felt this way before, right? Bummed out! I resolved to find some cheap land in town and build my own mini-storage facility. I knew it was going to be more expensive to build than to buy, but it seemed like the only option. I found a piece of land that was centrally located, then talked the seller down to less than half the original asking price. I talked with the city over the process of getting building plans approved and everything involved with that. I even met with a few builders to get opinions and bids on what the exact cost would be to build my ideal mini-storage facility.

During all this planning, I had one rainy day, a rainy day where not much work was getting done, and not much was happening in my social life. I decided to take one more chance, make one more drive around town. On this last drive around, I would try to find a mini-storage facility I had not contacted and would make a final effort to buy my way into the mini-storage business.

To my surprise, I found a 35-unit mini-storage facility right next to a Walmart.

HUSTLE

Then Repeat

I called the number on the sign and asked to speak directly with the owner.

I encouraged him—by Sucking up—to meet me at the property within the hour to discuss the terms of a purchase.

HUSTLE

Even more to my surprise, the owner didn't laugh at me, did not cuss me out, did not try to run me off. Instead, he spoke eight glorious words: "I will be there in 25 minutes." It might have been seven words, but I was too excited to count words.

I waited patiently in my car until the owner pulled up. Getting right to it, we haggled over the price for about a half hour, me shooting ridiculously low offers, and the owner getting more and more reasonable every minute. At the end of that 30-minute conversation, we shook

Then Repeat

hands. A deal had been made. Our next step was to get it on paper and send it to the title company for closing.

The best part of the deal was that the owner graciously agreed to finance almost half of the purchase price. Boy, was *that* music to my ears. All that Time and hard work searching for the right facility—the right facility for us—finally paid off. This was a lesson for me and a lesson for you that putting in the Time pays off. I didn't feel like a winner during all those rejections by other mini-storage owners, but I felt like an Olympic gold champion when I finally closed that deal for the mini-storage next to Walmart.

HUSTLE

Like me, you will often have to put in more hours than you want to count doing whatever it takes to grow your business, growing the diversification of your business and products.

They say Time is money, and lucky for us we have 24 hours every day for our use, to make our personal and professional dreams come true. How much Time are you willing to put in to get the results you need? Are you willing to put in the Time when others around you aren't?

Time may have limits, but you can become Limitless.

L.imitless

Salesmanship is Limitless. Our very living is selling. We are all salespeople.

James Cash Penney

It is inevitable that on the road to achieving your dreams and desires, people will doubt you. People will talk bad about you or say that what you want isn't realistic or even possible. Don't let those naysayers put limits on your potential. You truly have untapped potential to do whatever you want.

Don't let your own doubts and worries stop you, either. Steven Pressfield refers to those inevitable negative thoughts as Resistance, which always is "preceded by a Dream, a creative vision of something original and worthy that you or I might do or produce." That resistance, that doubt you experience, he says, is a clue that you are on the right track, bringing a dream into reality.

HUSTLE

After Britney and I purchased that mini-storage facility, we knew our next step was to continue to acquire real estate property to rent.

My friends and family who know me well know I can't pass up any good deal. I'm tempted constantly. Whether the good deals be cars, real estate, a fast food special, a buy one get one free smartphone, they all tempt me the same. Britney is sometimes less enthusiastic, I admit, but she is generally supportive.

Our next step was to push the limits of finding good deals. There weren't very many good deals on the active market in my area. All the good deals were either done off-market or got turned into a bidding war where the final price ended up not being such a good deal. Our local real estate market was hot, which made it hard to find good deals to purchase.

Although some say it would be nice if things were always easy, I liked the challenge that having no good deals on the market presented to me. My plan of action was to find off-market real estate deals and put them together without the competition of other realtors bidding the price up. That competition always is there when a new property hits the market in my town, like in all towns.

Then Repeat

Many people know this technique as cold calling, and many people don't like it. Cold calling is simply calling potential sellers who do not know they are potential sellers, who probably will not sell, especially not for the price I offered. This is what I did for the mini-storage property, calling many off-market mini-storage facilities to find that one person who was willing to sell.

I started by calling expired real estate listings, properties that had been listed but for some reason or another did not sell and were taken off the market. Honestly, cold calling is one of the last things I like to do, but I knew it was one way I could expand my business, so I sucked it up and got on the phone.

After making a lot of calls, I finally got a promising lead, an older man named Jerry who had a nice 3-bedroom, 2-bathroom, 2-car garage home listed that had expired and did not sell. I enquired about this house, only to find out he already sold it to someone else when it went off market, a dead end.

I was about to hang up, but something prompted me to ask, "Jerry, what else ya got?" That question made the difference. After thinking a few moments, Jerry said he had another house he might sell—for the right price. It was also a 3-bedroom, 2-bathroom, 2-car garage home in a

HUSTLE

good part of town. I assumed Jerry wanted big money for this property, that it may not be worth my Time, but I checked it out. This house had been a rental for years, so I assumed the home would be trashed. I assumed that Jerry, a wily old landlord, wouldn't budge from a top-dollar price.

I tried to set a meeting with Jerry to look at this property, but he got kind of dodgy and backed off. He ended the call and I went back to calling other expired listings. Over the next three days I called Jerry once a day. After the third call, Jerry finally committed to meet me at the house. I showed up early, because as a professional, I always show up early.

After walking through the house and running some numbers on my phone, I concluded the home was worth about $120k. Jerry and I had yet to talk about price, so I asked Jerry what his lowest dollar was. He replied firmly, $75,000. I was stunned. This 70-year-old man seemed stuck on property values from 30 years ago. I kept on my poker face and haggled him down a couple thousand more and ended up purchasing the home for $72k. The seller paid all closing costs, which saved me another $1,000.

Then Repeat

Here was the best part of this situation: since the property value was so much higher than the purchase price, I was able to borrow more than $20k above my purchase price. I ended up getting a 100 percent financing deal for this home and walked away with an extra $20K in my pocket.

This is what I mean by pushing the Limits of business. I felt so good about this situation that I started calling older landlords like Jerry in my town. My goal was to pinpoint older landlords who may be tired of dealing with old rentals and crappy tenants, or tired of fixing up old houses that keep falling apart. My goal was to find people in distress and make them offers they couldn't

HUSTLE

refuse. I kept doing what I despised the most, cold calling, except this time I wasn't just calling expired listings, I was focused, cold calling aging landlords who were ready for some relief. Britney and I ended up acquiring five more single-family rental homes just by calling retiring landlords and buying up the scraps they were no longer willing to deal with.

Again, your business and your success may not be in real estate, it could be in something completely different, but the principle still stands that there are man-made limits in your profession/business/workplace. You don't need to play by those rules. You don't need to play by the limits that have been set by people who came before you. You have no limits and your potential is endless. I fully believe that of you, because you're the type of person who reads books like this who then gets to work. You are motivated, you are extraordinary. You are Hungry.

Finally, another way I pushed my personal Limits was by setting a goal of making three offers to purchase real estate every single day. Whether it was an off-market property, a listing put on the market by a realtor, or a for-sale-by-owner, I made three offers a day consistently for several months. All my offers were low-priced, all my offers were AS-IS, NO INSPECTIONS, CLOSE

QUICKLY. Everything about my offers was appealing except for the purchase price.

I would like to share another success story after making those offers every day for months, but nothing came of it. Out of all of those offers I had spent many, many hours writing up, none were accepted. Not one. But I was trying, and that was important, trying to do my best to deserve the rewards I wanted.

What can you do to push your limits for your business or product? Are you willing to push the limits that society has set for you?

For some, the limits may be regular hours, the average workday. I knew a cable salesman who, instead of knocking doors during the daytime, knocked doors between 6 p.m. and 10 p.m. While his colleagues spent hours and hours of daylight getting rejected or getting no response, my friend knocked when no one else was knocking. He would annoy some people, sure, and get lots of "interrupted dinner" lectures, but what he found was that his prospects were home. They were not at work, not at school, they were home, right in front of his face where he had the opportunity to pitch his product.

By working outside normal business hours, he worked smarter. He still worked hard, of course,

HUSTLE

but only when his potential clients were likely to be home. Unorthodox? Intruding? Inconsiderate? Only to those who didn't buy. Those who did buy appreciated his efforts. He had become Limitless.

This cable salesman sold more than any of the other cable salesman who followed the routine, who did not push the limits of their business. He sold more because he was not only Limitless, he was Efficient.

E.fficient

One of the ways I think you make more money is by creating more Efficiency.

Jeff Bewke

If you knew me well, you would most likely have the same opinion that my family and friends have. I am possibly one of the two or three cheapest people you will ever meet. I've picked pennies off the ground for years and would just about starve rather than spend money eating out. I've always felt the need to be frugal, to save for things that matter most. Saving money has been ingrained in my inner being since I was 12, when I started saving up pennies and dimes for things I wanted.

The things that mattered most when I was 12 were a good set of longboarding wheels, a new pair of headphones, or maybe even an Airsoft™ gun. Now that I'm older, the things that matter most to me are different, but the principle is the same. I still save as part of everyday life to purchase what matters most. I still want cool headphones, sure, but that stuff can wait.

What mattered most to Britney and me as we grew our real estate empire was paying off our personal home.

Many people pay off the homes where they live, but many, many people don't. Of course, there are pros and cons to having the debt versus not having the debt. The biggest pro that Britney and I saw was if we paid off our home, we could apply for a Home Equity Line of Credit, a HELOC.

The difference between a normal home loan and a HELOC is that a HELOC is like a super huge credit card. It can be paid off and then used again at your own convenience. With a normal home loan, it takes a huge refinance process to borrow back money that you have previously paid to the bank while paying down your loan. On a HELOC, all you need is to walk inside the bank and tell them how much you want, up to the limits of your credit line, then they cut you a cashier's check.

I suggest you learn more about home equity lines of credit. They can improve your business and really push you farther in your growth than you thought imaginable.

Britney and I knew this was our next step, paying off our home loan so we could restructure into a HELOC. It was very hard, but we definitely received many blessings along the way. We scrimped and saved and sold things that we didn't necessarily need, all for the cause of paying off our home. We refinanced some of our rental properties to get more cash to pay down our personal home. I also worked like a dog selling real estate, helping buyers and sellers alike, generating commissions that we applied to our home loan.

In less than two years, we reached our goal of putting a HELOC on our home. All luxuries and many everyday amenities were sacrificed to achieve our goal. We saved by eating home-cooked meals, putting the car in neutral on hills to save gas, and picking pennies up off the ground.

HUSTLE

These frugal habits, along with some major blessings from God, pushed us to our goal. Whether you believe in God, another type of deity, a higher power or substance that seems to keep the whole universe together, most people admit there is an unseen force that attracts things we desire. If we speak positive things and do positive things and aspire to do greater, bigger positive things, we will receive positive things in life. On the contrary, if we think negatively all the time, second guess ourselves all the time, and think about negatives instead of positives, then it's a no brainer that we will receive a good amount of negativity in life.

Our reason for putting a HELOC on our home was for Efficiency. We knew that with the HELOC we could purchase properties for cash, HELOC cash. After purchasing the property for cash, we would fix it up and take the paid for property to a bank and get a long-term loan. We would use the long-term loan proceeds to pay back down our HELOC.

This is called the BRRRR Method, meaning Buy/Remodel/Rent/Refinance/Repeat. It's an easy way to cycle money through property and essentially get into an unlimited amount of property with no money down. This process only works if your all-in total cost of a property is 80 percent or less than its fair market value.

Let me explain.

It's important to know a few key things as we talk about this real estate investment method.

Key Pointer 1

Most banks will not loan you more than 80 percent of the property value if it is an investment property. This is called a loan-to-value or LTV ratio. Your all-in cost for a property should never exceed 80 percent of the value of that property, otherwise you will be out of pocket some money.

Key Pointer 2

Let's say you find a move-in ready house that is worth $100k. Let's say you lowball an offer on this house and purchase it for $80k cash. You then take the paid for rental house to a bank and ask to refinance that rental house. The bank will hire an appraiser to determine the value of the house. The appraisal will come back at $100k. The bank will then loan you 80 percent of the value of the home, which in this example is $80k. You just got back 100 percent of the money you had invested in that rental home. It gets even better, because your tenant's monthly rent

HUSTLE

payment to you makes the monthly bank payment. This means you literally got into a house with $0 down, and someone else makes the payment for you. If that's not Efficient, I don't know what is. If you do that 10 times, cycling the same $80k through properties valued at $100k, you have successfully created a million-dollar rental portfolio with only $80k.

Key Pointer 3

Not all homes you purchase with the BRRRR Method will be move-in ready, meaning no work needed. Often the property needs some work. For example, you find a house that would be worth $100k if it was fixed up. You crunch the numbers with your contractor and determine that the home needs $10k in repairs. You make a low-ball offer of $70k for the house. Let's say by some miracle your $70k offer gets accepted, then you do the $10k repairs to bring it to a $100k value, for a total of $80k cash invested. After the repairs, you Hustle and find a renter for the home. You would then go to your bank and refinance the house you put $70k plus $10k into. As long as that home is worth $100k on the appraisal, the bank will pay you 80 percent of the appraised value, or $80k. This means you just got paid back for 100 percent of the cash you had invested in that home.

Then Repeat

Of course, the BRRRR method can only sustain you and keep working for you as long as your local appraisers appraise your properties at their true value. Even though appraisers are supposed to be completely unbiased, and are supposed to know their jobs, in my experience many appraisers don't know what they are doing. Your appraisal can depend on whether the appraiser ate a good breakfast and has a happy stomach. Your appraisal may depend on whether the appraiser's spouse is mad or not. At least sometimes, many appraisers are kind of finicky in that their mood can influence the value of your appraisal.

In the early 2000s, you could almost tell an appraiser what the value of an appraised property needed to be, and he or she would set it at that value for you. Now, on the contrary, it seems most appraisers are under-appraising all properties and being conservative to the point of being unrealistic about the values they are setting on properties.

Britney and I had a personal encounter with this predicament when we went to refinance our mini-storage unit. The appraiser came in with an appraised value $60k less than what the value truly was. Even after I showed him comparable properties and disputed the appraisal for weeks,

HUSTLE

the appraiser was too stubborn to add the new info and update the value, leaving our appraised value at an extremely low number. I realized that the BRRRR Method only works if you get honest appraisers who know what they are doing.

If this is a method that you are considering in the future, steer clear of wacky appraisers.

The BRRRR Method can be a confusing concept to grasp and to execute. I did not understand it the first few times it was explained to me. I'd highly encourage you to search further into this method if you are thinking about getting into real estate or are already in real estate. It's a way for you to achieve faster growth.

Obviously, the hardest part is getting the lump sum of money to start, or in our case, paying off our home and putting a HELOC on it. These are the things that were Efficient for us and our situation. What is Efficient for you in your situation? There are many small business loans or small business credit lines available to companies or products that are just starting up/starting out, or even for seasoned companies looking for new growth.

Efficiency might be the most important practice you can have in your business. If you can learn and practice how to become Efficient when you have less, your growth will be exponential when you have more and continue to be Efficient. Efficiency may mean cutting costs, or increasing your budget, or changing up your product to make it more diverse or changing your product to make it more simple. You know what's right for your business. You can trust your gut feeling on what changes need to be done to be more Efficient in your production, your sale, and your execution.

I'll ask you one more time: What can you do to be Efficient in your business or product? Are you willing to put in the Time and effort it takes to become more Efficient in your business? As you find what works for you, can you Repeat it?

HUSTLE

R.epeat

With repetition, alternate approaches become clear, options open.

Robert Genn

The last principle of this book—but by far the most important—is, simply, Repeat.

Your temporal success will not be built on just one moment or one single transaction. The way to continual accomplishment and wealth is by Repeating these good principles over and over until you reach your current goal and move on to the next one.

The principle of Repeating is nothing new. We Repeat sleep every night. We Repeat exercise multiple times a week. We eat Repeatedly every single day. We go to school or to a job more than once. Most things of value require Repetition, the things that are worth the most to us.

Then Repeat

That is why it is crucial that we continue to Repeat the H.U.S.T.L.E. principles, over and over:

Hungry

Unthinkable

Suck up

Time

Limitless

Efficient

Repeating these principles in your everyday life—and especially in your business—will bring you not just one single instance of success but many instances of success.

Repeated success.

Here is our best example of how Britney and I Repeated every H.U.S.T.L.E. principle in one business transaction, our most recent rental home purchase.

It turned out to be a success—obviously—because we applied the principles of success.

HUSTLE

This is a picture of the home we purchased, which is in a fantastic location in Springfield, Missouri. Really, you couldn't get much better than this location. It was a fixer upper for sure, but the best deals are fixer uppers. Right? Fixer uppers provide you with a chance to get some sweat equity into the home and really personalize it to the type of investment property you want.

Hungry

First, I was Hungry in this situation. Leaving the office one day, a shared real estate office with a few coworkers, I turned to a fellow realtor. I asked whether he "had any good deals up his sleeve that might be a fixer upper, or any deals where the seller would entertain a lower cash offer." Such a question was way out of the blue

Then Repeat

for my relationship with this fellow realtor. He and I had chatted about life and bonded over dirt bikes and other vehicles, sure, but he didn't deal with the fixer upper type houses, focusing more on a higher-class clientele.

Nevertheless, I felt like giving it a go and just asked: "Whatcha got for me?"

That question made all the difference. That question opened the door to what would be one of the most successful deals that Britney and I have put together so far. My coworker said he did, in fact, have a deal coming up in the next few months that fit my criteria. Surprised, I asked him to keep me posted on the progress of the deal. Every week or two, I would talk to this coworker specifically about this upcoming deal. After three months of following up, the time came to put this deal together.

The property was a nice 4-bedroom, 2-bathroom, 2-car garage, almost 2,000-foot home in a desirable school district. I discovered the house needed quite a few repairs, including a new roof, new windows, paint throughout the house, new flooring in several sections, and an updated electrical box before it would pass inspection.

A lot of tree trimming and cleanup work were needed to improve the property's overall

HUSTLE

condition. Long story short, this house would be quite a lot to chew. But you know how you eat an elephant, right? One bite at a time! How else to do you eat an elephant? Start by being Hungry!

Unthinkable

Eventually, I realized that two cars sat untouched in the driveway the whole three months of negotiation. One vehicle was a 1993 Ford Ranger 5-speed transmission with a camper shell and a spare tire. It had either 99k miles or 199k miles, because older odometers just keep rolling over. The second vehicle was a 1996 Ford Aerostar, something you might see an old guy driving as he offers free candy to kids. The van had 216k miles, but a very clean interior, and a spare tire.

Because I had seen these cars in the driveway for so long, untouched, I asked the sellers if they would sell them. Obviously, the cars were not being used and I figured the sellers would rather go for the cash. The sellers considered, then said that they would take $200 per car, which is pretty much the scrap price. The Ford Ranger was worth maybe $2k and the Aerostar a similar amount.

During the negotiation process, a few other investors found out this home was for sale. My original offer was $65k, but these other investors started to make offers that were higher than mine. After that grueling process of a bidding war, Britney and I walked away triumphant, purchasing the home for $75,500. Since my wife and I had paid so much more than our original offer, I asked the sellers to throw in the cars and, while we were at it, all the contents of the house. Can you believe that? Buying a house and taking the cars along with it? LOL. Included in the house was an assortment of furniture, couches, tables, dining room tables, lounging chairs, old televisions, ceiling fans, cabinets, an old treadmill, several weed cutters and blowers, a self-propelled mower, an old wood stove, and a refrigerator.

There were many more household items that had value and could be sold for cash. We had paid a little more for the home than we wanted, but we could make back most if not all that money by selling the contents of the home and the two cars. I was doing the Unthinkable. Again! Who thinks about buying someone's lounging chair when buying their home? Who thinks about keeping the toilet paper? Me! I took that TP home so I wouldn't have to buy some for a while. Doing this Unthinkable thing is part of what pushed my wife and me and gave us the extra cash we needed to start and maintain the remodel we had in mind for this property.

HUSTLE

Suck up

Buying this house was the kind of deal I live for. What really got my blood pumping was that I did not have enough cash to make the deal happen. Britney and I only had access to two-thirds of the purchase price, or $50k. The rest of our cash from our home equity line-of-credit, HELOC, was tied up in another real estate investment. What would we do? We needed to come up with $25k in just a couple of weeks. I thought about selling my nice Toyota pickup, and liquidating another few of our personal items. But that was my last resort, only if needed. I decided there was a better way.

I decided not to sell any of the things that I love and use every day. This new plan involved Sucking up to a private-party/hard-money lender here in town. Britney and I needed this money desperately, as it was the boost necessary to solidify the purchase of our next rental home. We reached out to this private lender, who had loaned us money in the past, at a reasonable interest rate. Since our current situation was a little impulsive and we were asking for the cash almost immediately, I decided to tailor my business proposition to this particular lender and make it as appealing to him as possible. I promised an interest rate that was considerably higher than I had paid in the past and promised a 60-day fast turnaround of the lender's cash. With those two promises, the lender decided to loan the money. Britney and I were able to close the deal on this new home and pick up some cars and personal belongings in the process. Had I not Sucked up to this private lender, I would not have gotten the funds needed to close the deal. It's so important to take care of other people so they will take care of you.

Time

Some deals go very quickly, while others are more drawn out. This deal took almost three months, which is quite a bit of Time. Usually, real-estate deals can be put together in 30 days or less. When a deal is with cash, meaning no bank financing is necessary to make the transaction

HUSTLE

close, they can go even more quickly, in as little as two or three days. Nevertheless, three months—almost 90 days—was a good chunk of Time.

During this Time I was patient. I followed up frequently with my coworker who was helping the seller put this deal together. Between my weekly follow up and the Time and effort put into the deal by my coworker, everything ran smoothly and according to plan. I also ended up having quite a bit of Time invested shortly after the deal, while selling the items left in the house, some selling as cheap as $25 and as expensive as $2,000. At various points it didn't feel like it was worth it to run all the way across town just to meet someone and sell them an end table for $25, but at the end of the day when I tallied up all the money Britney and I made from selling those personal effects, it was well in the thousands. At that point, it was worth it.

Considerable Time was spent checking up with the title company on this deal and buttering up my private lender. More Time was spent getting a termite inspection just to make sure we weren't going to be in over our heads with unexpected repairs.

Putting in the Time is worth it, part of your due diligence. However, it is vital to know that just putting in Time does not necessarily mean you are being productive. Be cautious, protective of your Time. It is easy to sometimes work harder, not smarter, instead of vice versa.

Limitless

You might be wondering: what unorthodox thing did Mike do in this deal to be Limitless? What kind of crazy stuff can be done with a house that needs remodeled, a few junk cars, and a bunch of furniture? First and foremost, as you know, Britney and I sold the things that were left behind. What you don't know is that not all were sold for cold, hard cash.

Our tool inventory was three weed cutters, two identical leaf blowers, a Craftsman™ self-propelled mower, and a few odds and ends for yard work. I listed every single item in Facebook Marketplace, and stuff started moving quickly. The first thing to go was the couch, then the refrigerator.

I got a message from a guy wanting one of the leaf blowers, listed for $85, almost half of the original price. He offered $70, which I accepted if he would pick it up that night. While I was chatting with this guy on Messenger, the Kansas City Chiefs were winning Super Bowl LIV. After that great game, I met up with this guy at

HUSTLE

9:45 p.m. We met at the rental home Britney and I had just purchased and fired up the leaf blower just to prove that it did, in fact, work.

As he loaded the leaf blower into his truck, he mentioned he was starting a lawn care/tree cutting business. This triggered an idea. There were several trees in the front yard of this new rental home that needed to be taken down. City Utilities and my insurance agent both had warned us about those severely overhanging branches. The going rate for tree cutting in our town was roughly $500 per tree, and I had four trees and one stump that needed to be removed. I asked what he would charge to do the job. After analyzing it for a few minutes, he said $400. I thought, "Hmm, $400 a tree? That's a little less than the going rate." To my surprise, he said, "For $400, I'll take all the trees down."

I couldn't believe it. This guy would do the work for less than a $100 per tree. I was ecstatic! I was ready to pay him the cash and have the trees removed. Then I had another thought. This guy is starting a lawn work/yard work/tree trim business. No doubt he would need more tools as he grows his business. I heard these words coming out of my mouth: "I will give you three weed cutters, valued at $95 each, plus another blower worth $90. That's a $375 value, and I'll

Then Repeat

throw in $100 cash just to make the deal sweeter for you. That's $475 total, part in cash and the remainder in tools."

Those weed cutters and leaf blower were *sold*, but not for cold, hard cash. They were sold for labor hours. This gentleman liked the deal and we shook hands. We agreed to meet at the property three days later to start the work and get him compensated. In the back of my mind I was screaming. I couldn't believe I was trading some tools I got for free for a job that was worth almost $2,000. This was a complete slam dunk and a huge blessing. Three days later, we met up and got the job done.

This guy did such a good job removing the trees that I made him another proposition. That Craftsman™ self-propelled mower was still in the garage and there was still more lawn work to be done at the new rental to boost curb appeal.

I offered to trade him the mower plus some cash to spruce up the whole rest of the yard and take care of the little shrubs and a few other trees that needed cut down. The mower was worth about $190 and the cash would cover his time and the dump fees. He accepted my proposition and got to work.

HUSTLE

Britney and I were clearing out all these tools and getting great lawn work in return. I was so excited. There is value in everything, right, which leads to our next blessing.

Somehow, I had completely forgotten there was a 23x12 storage building in the back yard. This little building had a recent paint job, a newer 3-Tab shingle roof, and was clean as can be inside. When I first walked through the home before purchasing it, I did not think much of the shed. I figured the eventual renters would appreciate the shed and use it to store their tools. But now, after purchasing the home, I realized we would be better off selling this shed outright for cash. I was overjoyed that this was yet another asset we could liquidate to fund the remodel on this new rental home.

I quickly got online and Googled how much a new shed of this caliber would cost. I checked local Facebook classifieds to see what used sheds were selling for. I wanted to price the shed accurately and get top dollar in a reasonable amount of time. I was shocked! Sheds of this type, size, and condition were going for $3,500 new, and used for between $1,500 and $2,500. I decided to list it for $1,950 and stay firm, as this seemed like a fair price. Sheds listed for $2,500 had been on the market for months, but I didn't want to wait that long hoping to make a few extra bucks. It was worth more to me to price it at exactly what it was worth and move it, you know, to get it off the lot.

I took some super cute, detailed pictures of the shed, inside and out. I posted the shed for sale on many Facebook groups as well as Facebook marketplace. Within several hours, I had seven people lined up, wanting to buy it, even though I had posted late at night. I woke up the next morning to multiple other individuals wanting to buy this utility building. I couldn't believe it. Storage sheds were more of a hot commodity than I had figured.

It was snowing heavily that morning, with a couple inches on the ground, so most people were unable to pick it up that day. I had one guy, though, who was super interested in the storage shed. He really wanted it! He was head-over-heels and said he would come pay for the building that very day then pick it up when the weather cleared. He couldn't get off work to meet me right away, so he called his retired father, who went to the bank and pulled out the cash. He met me over at the house and paid full price, $1,950.

In less than 24 hours, I had sold this shed and gotten my asking price. Britney and I were thousands of dollars ahead at this point, including

HUSTLE

the items we sold from this home. Pushing the limits of your local market and pushing your personal limits may be challenging, but doing so will ultimately grow your business, and set you up for increased success.

On top of this, I spoke to every contractor we had at that house and tried to pitch them on the possibility of trading the 1993 Ford Ranger or the 1996 Ford Aerostar—or both—for labor. None of the contractors accepted my proposition, but it was worth a shot. Being Limitless often means pushing your own personal boundaries and doing something that might otherwise make you uncomfortable or embarrassed. Being Limitless in your business is crucial if you're going to have the success you so greatly desire.

Efficiency

Knowing that Britney and I had three months of negotiation and preparation before purchasing this property, what do you think we did? We organized a plan on how we were going to remodel it before we even bought it. Our remodel plan included the when, the how, the how much, and the specific contractors who were going to work for us. We had every detail hammered out to the penny.

We decided it would be most Efficient to hit the ground running immediately after we purchased the property. Luckily, the sellers were gracious enough to allow us access to the home before the closing day so we could bag up trash and clean out the home. We did this to get it completely ready so our contractors could start work right after closing. I personally bagged up dozens of garbage bags full of trash, old clothes, old printers, and old books. This was really Efficient.

I also took a leap of faith regarding the new windows we would install. Weeks before we had even closed, trusting that the home would close with no issues, I ordered a dozen new windows. I paid for the windows before paying for the house. The worker at Lowes who helped me order the windows asked me twice if I was sure I wanted to buy windows without knowing whether my deal was going to close.

I knew that custom windows would take weeks to arrive, and I knew if I waited until after closing I would be set back four or five weeks before we would receive the windows. I wanted to order the windows right away so we could hit the ground running and install them shortly after closing.

Fast forward a few weeks. We closed on the home. Yay!

That same day I had my roofer, who I had already received a bid from and scheduled for the day of closing, come put a roof on the home.

Then Repeat

As soon as the roof was completed, my electrician came to update the electric panel to a new breaker box as opposed to the old fuse box.

Before our first full day of ownership was over, we already had a new roof and a new electrical box. The windows were set to install just a few days after the closing.

We also had full-time handymen around-the-clock busting out the painting, wallpaper removal, flooring installation, carpet removal, trash removal, plumbing and drywall repairs, and everything else the home needed. We had a handyman who worked during normal working hours. We had a crew of two or three handymen who worked the night shift. Between these two crews, our Efficiency skyrocketed.

Britney and I were not willing to drag our feet. Our goal was to get in—and out of—the house as quick as possible, remodeled and rented out as soon as possible.

After renting it out, we would apply the BRRRR Method—Buy/Remodel/Rent/ Refinance/Repeat—and refinance it to pull our cash back out of the property. It is through Efficiency that you GET STUFF DONE.

There it is, H.U.S.T.L.E. then Repeat.

HUSTLE

I wish for you to make good deals happen in your business, over and over. Never be satisfied with just one good deal or one good sales pitch.

Repeat these principles again and again and again and again until you have so much success that you don't even know how to handle it. Then write your own book.

Have so much success that you get tired of all the success you are having.

Now, Push Your Snowball

Forget yourself, and go to work.

Bryant Hinckley

You have now read our story, so far, on how we have pushed the snowball of success. Know that every situation is different, that every business or product has its own trials and errors.

Know that as you apply the H.U.S.T.L.E. principles—*Hungry, Unthinkable, Suck Up, Time, Limitless, Efficient*—then *Repeat*—your success will grow, and you will get the results you so desperately desire.

I wouldn't feel right without acknowledging that God has had an immense, consistent hand in my life, in our lives, including our business successes. He wants to bless you, too. All you need is to give Him a reason to.

HUSTLE

God helps those who help themselves. It is as we do all that we can that He lends a helping hand.

"For if there be no faith among the children of men God can do no miracle among them; wherefore, he showed not himself until after their faith."

Ether 12:12

You have the drive, you have the motivation. That's one reason you are reading this book. Keep it handy and reread it often.

Now put down the book and get to work.

Then Repeat

Before You Go, Leave a Review

If you found this book useful or otherwise enjoyable, tell your family, friends, and coworkers. That's what Facebook, Twitter, and Instagram are for, right?

Please follow this link to leave a review on Amazon. I will read and consider what you say, because I want to provide the best books I can. Your input helps.

Follow this link:

https://www.amazon.com/dp/B085X7KBDR

Thank you again for buying this book.

Now, show us what you can do when you HUSTLE.

HUSTLE

Made in the USA
Monee, IL
03 February 2021